Recent Explorations In The Wappinger Valley Limestones And Other Formations Of Dutchess County, New York

W. B. Dwight

In the interest of creating a more extensive selection of rare historical book reprints, we have chosen to reproduce this title even though it may possibly have occasional imperfections such as missing and blurred pages, missing text, poor pictures, markings, dark backgrounds and other reproduction issues beyond our control. Because this work is culturally important, we have made it available as a part of our commitment to protecting, preserving and promoting the world's literature. Thank you for your understanding.

[FROM THE AMERICAN JOURNAL OF SCIENCE, VOL. XXXVIII, AUGUST, 1889.]

RECENT EXPLORATIONS IN THE WAPPIN-
GER VALLEY LIMESTONES AND OTHER
FORMATIONS OF DUTCHESS CO., N. Y.

BY W. B. DWIGHT.

[FROM THE AMERICAN JOURNAL OF SCIENCE, VOL. XXXVIII, AUGUST, 1889.]

RECENT EXPLORATIONS IN THE WAPPINGER VALLEY LIMESTONES AND OTHER FORMATIONS OF DUTCHESS CO., N. Y.

By W. B. Dwight.

No. 7. *Fossiliferous Strata of the Paradoxides Zone at Stissing.*

THE occurrence of fossiliferous Cambrian strata of the Potsdam group near Poughkeepsie, N. Y., and ten miles north of that city at Salt Point, has been described in previous papers of this series:* also the discovery by Mr. C. D. Walcott and myself, in a joint trip, of fossiliferous strata of the Olenellus horizon on the southern extremity of Stissing Mountain, 21

---

* This Journal, Feb., 1886, and July, 1887.

miles north of Poughkeepsie. It is the object of this paper to present a few of the prominent results of my more recent researches in the Cambrian and associated strata in that part of the county adjacent to Stissing Mountain.

The particular aim of these later investigations has been to ascertain the position and extent of the Olenellus strata, and their stratigraphic relations to the Hudson River shales of the region, and to the higher Cambrian strata whose presence a few miles to the southward had been already demonstrated.

The Olenellus quartzite and the overlying Olenellus limestone, rest upon the gneiss of Stissing Mountain around the entire circuit of its southern extremity and so continue northeastward for several miles along both its eastern and western flanks. At the southern extremity, about 2½ miles northeasterly from Poughkeepsie, these strata cover the basal slopes of the mountain at an elevation of about 275 feet above the adjoining valleys and, conforming to these slopes, lie with a very gentle inclination to the south. On descending the slopes in southerly directions, the upper layers of the Olenellus limestone are found to run frequently into red shales which have not proved fossiliferous. In the fields which stretch southward and southwestward from the mountain, the rocks are to a great extent concealed by drift; but there are a sufficient number of outcrops to permit a continuous tracing of the limestones and calcareous shales (of whatever horizon they may be) for several miles, and to show that the dip rapidly increases, and the strike soon becomes the prevailing one of about N. 20° to 30° E. On account of the cover of drift, and the scarcity of fossils, it is at present impossible to determine exactly, along what lines the Olenellus group is succeeded by strata of later periods.

This mass of limestones of the Olenellus and to the southward probably of higher groups, which extends in the line of strike southwestward, is abruptly cut off on the west by a fault caused by the uplift of a belt of Olenellus quartzite, overlain on the west by a strip of limestone of the same age. West of this limestone are the shales of the Hudson River group. This fault begins at a point between two and three miles southwest of Mt. Stissing, where, however, only the limestone at first appears, faulting on the east (as well as the west) against Hudson River shale. This line of fault extends in a direction a little east of north to western flank of the mountain. One of the best places to observe it is one mile west from Stissing Station, on the road leading west beyond the corner of the McIntyre road, near Mr. Elias Turner's house. At this point the quartzite comes in, as a bold conspicuous ledge of white unfossiliferous rock. From this point northeastward, the quartzite faults against the Olenellus and associated limestones on the east, while it is bordered on the west by a belt, from 800 to 1000 feet wide in its outcrop of overlying limestone, partly at least of the Olenellus group.

After reaching the mountain, this belt follows along its flanks to Miller's Pond, during which course, the Hudson River shales on the west pinch out the limestone and rest against the quartzite for about 700 feet. North of Miller's Pond, the Olenellus belt begins to ascend the mountain flanks, until at a point about half a mile south of the "gap," the limestone entirely disappears, and the quartzite pressed upon by the Hudson River Shales stands out in bold white crags high up the mountain side,—at perhaps two-thirds of its height. North of this point, the Hudson River shales apparently rest directly upon the gneiss.

On the east side of Mount Stissing, the Olenellus belt does not tend at any point to climb its flanks; the tendency is rather to sheer away from them. The quartzite is here mainly on the west side of the belt. At a point, however, opposite to Attlebury Station, where there is a deep recess to the west in the outline of the mountain, there is a synclinal of limestone and calcareous shales lying west of the quartzite and filling up the gap.

At Mr. J. A. Thompson's house at the turn in the road northeast of Attlebury Station, the quartzite disappears in the meadows while the Olenellus limestone forms a bold escarpment along the base of the mountain, west of the road, for about half-a-mile farther north. Opercula of *Hyolithellus micans* occur in this limestone opposite Mr. Thompson's house. From this point the belt, much concealed by drift and alluvium, passes northeastwardly by and under the village of Pine Plains to the county line. There are outcrops of the quartzite in Mr. Henry Pitcher's swamp, north of the village, and on top of a hill belonging to Mrs. Henry Hoffman, and on the south side of the road close to the county line, near Mr. J. Weaver's house. There are outcrops of limestone in the plain near the north extremity of Stissing Mountain, which probably belong to this group, but this is uncertain. It may here be remarked that the Hudson River Shales mount to the summit of that part of the mountain lying north of the "gap," at least in its northern portion. Also that the only other place where I have found quartzite referable to the Olenellus group in this part of the county is a ledge in a ravine on Wing's farm a little southwest of the station at Willow Brook.*

---

* My explorations around Pine Plains were much facilitated by the generous assistance of Rev. A. Mattice, principal of Seymour Smith Institute.

Besides the strata already mentioned, there are limestones filling the eastern side of the valley east of the mountain, cropping out in Thomas's quarry on the northeastern edge of Pine Plains village, forming Mill Hill on its eastern edge, and other hills easterly as far as Bethel, and (in conjunction perhaps with the quartzite-limestone Olenellus belt,) passing north into Columbia County; also forming a belt about six miles long, and from a quarter of a mile to a mile wide in the Shekomeko valley, from Pulver's Corners on the north, to "The Square," two miles south of Shekomeko Station; also a very irregular strip about one mile and three quarters long and from a quarter of a mile to a mile in width, north of Bangall. All these outcrops I have searched and studied in detail, and have found them to be Cambro-Ordovician strata, much faulted against each other, and against the Hudson River Shales, especially in the Bangall strip. No Trenton outcrops have been found. Fossiliferous Calciferous strata occur at Attlebury Station, near the Moravian monument, at Bethel, and quite extensively at and south of Shekomeko.

The greater part of these limestones are Cambrian in appearance, passing very frequently into the calcareous shales characteristic of that zone in this county. But no fossils except those of the Calciferous strata have been found in any of the belts just named with the exception of a single fragment. This was found at the base of Mill Hill in Pine Plains Village, and may be either a Kutorgina or a Lingulepis. It is therefore at present impossible to determine the eastern edge of the Olenellus strata in the neighborhood of Pine Plains, or to distinguish, in this vicinity, the higher Cambrian strata, except in the single instance which will now be mentioned. It can scarcely be doubted, however, that the Potsdam zone is largely represented in connection with the Calciferous. The deep cutting on the railroad just north of Husted station is most probably in the Potsdam.

In July, 1887 the search in the limestones and calcareous shales immediately overlying the Olenellus limestone at the south end of Stissing Mountain was rewarded by the discovery of two or three fossils. No fossiliferous layer was then found; the organisms obtained were referred to the Potsdam zone which was to be expected in that position. It was not until the summer of 1888 that, by the discovery of a fossiliferous layer at this spot, the true significance of these important organisms began to appear.

The locality is in the first rock-cutting on the New York and Massachusetts Railroad, a little less than half a mile south of Stissing station. The organisms have been found chiefly in a thin layer of limestone and calcareous shales close to the ground and to the railroad track, near the southern end of the cut, and are more abundant in the shale. Roadmaster Joseph D. Neal very kindly put at my disposal a gang of the railroad employees to make the necessary excavation. Mr. Palmateer, who has charge of this "section," rendered very efficient service in conducting the work, and showed much skill in detecting fossils.

The species collected consists of a trilobite, a Leperditia, and a Kutorgina, all undescribed, and a Hyolithes, probably "Billingsi." As the latter has a large geological range, it would scarcely indicate the horizon, but the other organisms appear definitely to indicate the Paradoxides horizon in their character and affinities. Well defined specimens are very rare, and have been procured only by breaking up a large quantity of rock; but in certain thin layers, fragments of these fossils are very numerous. On account of the covering of soil, it is impossible to determine the boundary line between these Paradoxides beds, and those known to be of the Olenellus group, three quarters of a mile north on Stissing Mountain. It is probable however that the outcrop in the gulley at the station is of the latter group. It is equally impossible at present to determine the division line between these Paradoxides beds and the Potsdam strata doubtless overlying them, which latter are entirely similar in lithological characteristics.

No other locality of fossils of the Paradoxides horizon has yet been found. The only fossils of Paradoxides types previously reported from New York State, are those found by Mr. C. D. Walcott of the U S. Geological Survey, which he states that he is inclined to refer to the Paradoxides zone.* I have not been able to find any of these in the Stissing locality.

It may be observed that the stratigraphic position of the Stissing Paradoxides fauna is in harmony with the view which now seems likely to meet with general acceptance, that if the Olenellus and Paradoxides faunæ are not synchronous, the former should be regarded as the earlier deposit. It gives me pleasure to acknowledge the very kind and valuable assistance of Mr. C. D. Walcott in determining the relations of my specimens to typical Cambrian fossils.

A description of the species determined is here appended.

Hyolithes Billingsi? Plate VI, fig. 1.

About half a dozen tubes of Hyolithes have been found in the calcareous shale: they are from eight to twelve millimeters in length, and from three to four in diameter at the aperture. Most of them are poorly preserved, showing little more than a

---

* This Journal, III, vol. xxxvii, 1889, pp. 385, 387.

black flattened cone. In one specimen, the shell shows considerable thickness. The one figured is the best one found, though it is the internal cast, the shell being entirely exfoliated. The shape is an acute cone very slightly convex on the visible surface, and with a few evident annulations in the upper half, the most marked one being next to the aperture. The shape of the transverse section is unknown, though it has been sought for by making cross-sections.

A single operculum has been found, but it is not sufficiently perfect to warrant its description. This fossil may be most safely referred to *H. Billingsi*. Specimens of the above named species, kindly loaned to me for examination by Mr. C. D. Walcott, show distinctly the annulations which appear in the Stissing fossils.

Leperditia ebenina, n. sp. Plate VI, figs. 2, 3 and 4.

Carapace jet-black, shining, subelliptical; about eight millimeters long, and five millimeters high in the largest specimens collected. Dorsal margin straight, or nearly so, somewhat shorter than the longest diameter of the carapace. Ventral margin arcuate; terminal margins well-rounded ventrally, but above sloping inward, in straight lines, to the dorsal margin; dorsal angles somewhat obtuse, not at all rounded.

The carapace in general is quite convex; in the largest specimens, as in one of those here figured (fig. 3), there is a broad and rather flat depression passing centrally from the dorsal to the ventral edge, leaving two terminal prominences; but as in such cases cracks are evident in the shell, and as the smaller specimens do not exhibit this feature, it is probably the result of compression. On account of the imperfection of the specimens, and the frequent distortion by pressure, it is not at present possible to determine the normal outlines of surface convexity.

The external surface of the carapace is very peculiarly ornamented. The entire border of each valve, in the form of a strip which is nearly two millimeters wide in the largest specimens, is covered with extremely minute contiguous pits. There are at least from 100 to 150 to a square millimeter. Within this finely-pitted border, the entire central portion is covered with much larger, separated pits, the interspaces being as wide as the pits themselves, or wider. Their disposition is very irregular, but they average about 15 or 20 to the square millimeter. There is a linear marginal groove extending along the ventral border; at its central point it is nearly one millimeter within the ventral margin, but it gradually approaches it toward each extremity until it coalesces with the terminal margins. The central portions of the internal surface of the valves are covered with well-defined scattered tubercles, corresponding apparently with the scattered pits of the external surface.

No eye-tubercle nor muscle-spot is visible. Further particulars, as to relative obliquity of the dorsal angles, etc., cannot be ascertained until more perfect specimens are collected. In specimen No. 175, the valve appears to be a little wider on the left-hand than on the right-hand; it is therefore probable that the specimen is the right valve.

Found chiefly in the calcareous shale, but occasionally in the compact limestone. Some surfaces of the shale are black with its fragments, but owing to its brittleness no perfect specimens has been yet obtained.

Kutorgina Stissingensis, n. sp. Plate VI, figs. 5, 6, 7 and 8.

Shell black, phosphatic, slightly transverse; width about three-tenths greater than the length. Those collected from the limestone are about eight millimeters in width; specimens found in the calcareous shale are sometimes from eleven to twelve millimeters wide or even more. General shape, semicircular.

The cardinal margin slopes forward somewhat on each side of the beak, and makes obtuse angles with the lateral margins, on account of the incurving of the latter. It is shorter than the greatest width of the shell which is along a transverse line one-third of the distance from the beak to the front. Hingeline not evident, but apparently a little curved.

The ventral valve has the beak elevated, pointed, and projecting somewhat behind the cardinal margin. From the beak the surface slopes down toward each lateral margin, and to the front margin, becoming sometimes slightly concave at the central portions of the shell. Along the cardinal border the shell is suddenly deflexed, making a distinct false area which, however, is separated into two parts by a vacant deltidial space under the beak. As the surface of this false area is exfoliated in specimens observed, it cannot be positively determined whether the surface ornamentation of the valve is extended over it. The edge between the false area and the upper surface of the valve is not sharp, but gently rounded.

The dorsal valve is depressed and nearly flat, beak low; otherwise resembles the ventral valve, except that in specimens collected it appears a little more transverse.

The surfaces of both valves are covered with very fine, sharp, concentric ridges, traversed by striæ scarcely visible to the naked eye. Under a strong triplet these striæ prove to be very delicate longitudinal undulations radiating from the beak.

The concentric ridges are somewhat wavy as seen under a strong magnifier; they are semi-circular; a number of those lying nearest to the front margin, run out along the upper part of the lateral margins; but the remainder, and larger number terminate in regular order along the cardinal border. In front of the central portions of the shell, the concentric ridges, which number about 12 to 15 to a millimeter, are regularly concentric; but nearer to the beak the number, and the irregularity greatly increase. At a point about one-third the length of the shell, from the beak, there are twenty-five or more to the millimeter; as the radiating plications are numerous in this part, there is caused a complexity of curves, which under a powerful magnifier produces the effect of elegant and delicate basket work. The radiating undulations are very irregular in position and number, they are not thoroughly continuous from the beak, in specimens observed, but appear at irregular intervals singly or in groups; while apt to be crowded around the beak, they are rare near the front margin. On the best specimens, about 25 have been counted in the central parts of the shell just forward of the beak; had they extended in equal distribution around it, quite to the cardinal border, there would have been about 50. They are also unequal in breadth; where they are somewhat regular, the interspaces about equal the plications in width; these plications are multiplied by implantation.

The following internal markings are indicated by the study of a specimen (fig. 8,) which is supposed to be an umbonal fragment of a ventral valve of a *Kutorgina Stissingensis*, from the same locality.

The original specimen is a natural impression of the interior. The figure is drawn from a gutta-percha cast of the same, which therefore represents accurately the interior of the valve. In front of the deltidial groove, a thin medial septum extends toward the front. Lying close to this septum and divided by it, there is a posterior and an anterior pair of circular muscular impressions, separated from each other by a broad and low transverse ridge. Fine radiating lines extend out from along the septum, the front ones making a small angle with the latter, while the more posterior ones start out from the septum in a lateral direction, but are soon deflected into their proper radial position.

It is not quite certain that this latter fossil is identical with *K. Stissingensis*. It is an example of rather numerous organisms found at this locality, which for some time I supposed to be a new species of Lingulella, allied to *L. ella*. But as its surface-ornamentation appears to be quite exactly that of the *K. Stissingensis*, and for other reasons, I am now inclined to think that these little shells are either the young, or else fragmentary portions near the beak, of *L. Stissingensis*.

In the above description I have associated in the same species the specimens found in the calcareous shale, and those found in the compact limestone. There are some points of difference, especially in size; those in the shale are decidedly larger than those in the limestone, which may be due to more congenial sediment. The number found in the limestone however is too small to justify any strong conviction on this point.

Should it be ascertained hereafter that there are specific differences between these fossils, I should consider the specific name here given to belong to the specimens found in the limestone of which those corresponding to figs. 5 and 6 are the types.

Fragments of the front portion of this black shell are abundant and conspicuous in the shale, and in the absence of the associated fossils would readily be mistaken for fragments of *Lingulepis pinniformis*. Close inspection will however reveal this difference. The concentric ridges or laminae of *L. pinniformis* (at least as exhibited in Dutchess County, N. Y.) are feebly defined when magnified, and often run together obscurely; while those of *Kutorgina Stissingensis* as viewed with a strong triplet, are deeply cut, and in the front portions even, they are generally individualized with exquisite perfection.

This Kutorgina is related to *K. Labradorica* Billings; but the beaks are less elevated than the specimens figured of that species, and the peculiar surface ornamentation is different.

Olenoides Stissingensis, n. sp. Plate VI, figs. 9–15.

Body elongate ovate; in the single full-length specimen found, slightly over three centimeters in length.

Head large, semicircular, with apparently slight notches in the anterior outline, at the points of intersection with the facial suture. Eyes elongate and large.

Glabella elongate, its length in front of the occipital furrow, being nearly one and two thirds times its least width; a little expanded at the rounded anterior extremity, the sides slightly incurved along the posterior half, so that the shortest transverse diameter is a little in front of the posterior extremity. Dorsal furrow everywhere well defined, though not deep; inclined to be rather broad along the lateral edges. Glabellar furrows three, or in some specimens, four; the first pair are broadly and deeply impressed in the edges of the glabella, at a point about one-fourth of the longitudinal diameter from the posterior extremity; from here they pass very obliquely backward, shallowing and narrowing rapidly, until quite near to the posterior margin, they are joined by a shallow transverse furrow. The second pair arising from the central points in the edges are almost as oblique as the first pair and quite similar, except that they are slightly narrower, and considerably shorter, each one extending but a third of the distance across the glabella; the third and fourth furrows are very short and slight, often barely perceptible, and their direction is either directly transverse, or turned slightly forward.

Occipital furrow strongly defined at its outer extremities, where it terminates in pit-like depressions, but it is narrow, and very shallow toward the center.

Occipital ring, triangular, depressed convex, lower than the the glabella, very broad centrally, narrowing rapidly toward the lateral terminations; the postero-lateral margins pass directly to the fixed cheeks as elevated ridges, with only a slight transverse depression in the line of the occipital furrow. The occipital ring terminates posteriorly in an obtuse point. No occipital spine has been detected in specimens favorable for its exhibition if one were present.

The facial suture anteriorly passes obliquely forward and outward, in a sigmoid curve, from the anterior corner of the eye; from the posterior corner of the same, it runs nearly parallel to the posterior margin, until it turns and cuts this margin near the cheek-spine.

The fixed cheeks are broad, convex, elevated, but lower than the glabella; there is a deep furrow just within the well-marked palpebral-lobes; posterior limb with nearly parallel margins, and about as long as the shortest transverse diameter of the glabella; its furrow is broad and central at the inner end, but passes obliquely forward, as it vanishes before reaching the extremity. Front limb narrow, sloping upward from the dorsal furrow, elevated and rounding over at the margin; its contour is a curve of somewhat longer radius than that of the anterior outline of the glabella. Ocular ridge narrow and prominent, semicircular, extending anteriorly to the glabella at a point near the anterior end between the third and fourth furrows.

Free cheeks not well preserved in specimens collected; exclusive of the moderately long genal spine, their form is triangular, and the surface generally convex, rising towards the palpebral lobes. In the best preserved specimens there appears to be a narrow, flat, depressed margin, running down somewhat into the spine; from the anterior part of this margin, a deep furrow extends obliquely posteriorly, and inward, till it meets the posterior margin near the genal angle; it thus cuts off a strip of the convex portion of the cheek, which strip passes down into the spine to its point.

Hypostoma triangular, convex, well-rounded anteriorly, and the curved outline extending backward for more than $\frac{1}{8}$ of the distance along the sides; from this point, the sides are nearly straight, except at the posterior end, where there is an expansion into a broad, rounded, well-marked annulation, whose outlines are everywhere curved. Between the ring and the main body is a transverse, linear, deeply impressed furrow. There is a pair of short faint furrows, together forming a V, just in front of the posterior transverse furrow on each side.

From the central point of the front edge, a broad moderately deep furrow, extends a short distance backward, rapidly contracting to a vanishing point; it obscurely divides the anterior part of the hypostoma into two lobes. There is anteriorly, a narrow, rounded margin whose contour conforms to that of the front edge of the principal mass. It is uncertain from the partially imbedded specimens, whether or not, this margin extends also along the sides.

The thorax contains eight segments. Axis well-elevated, strongly convex, rate of taper regular, about one part in six. Each segment is of about the same width as the corresponding pleural segment, exclusive of the free spinous portion.

A linear furrow, deeply impressed, passing from one posterior corner to the other, traverses each segment through its central point. This furrow thus presents the shape of an arc convex anteriorly. Immediately behind its central and highest point there is a tubercle, or perhaps the base of a spine. All that portion of each segment lying within, and posterior to the furrow, presents a visible contrast to the anterior portion by some slight difference in the texture of its surface, which, for one thing, is a little the rougher; in the two specimens collected, it is also of a darker color. The pleural segments are depressed convex, and extend out very nearly at right angles to the central line of the axis, until the free spinous portions are reached. Each of the pleuræ consists of a broad, flat depressed portion or furrow, flanked by narrow, well-defined marginal ridges. The furrow is broad at its inner end, and continues of equal width for half the distance, when it rapidly draws down to a point. The posterior pleural ridge is almost perfectly straight through its entire length; the anterior ridge is straight for about half its length, while it lies appressed against the posterior ridge of the next segment in front; from this point it is at first gently, then rapidly recurved until it meets in an acute point the posterior ridge of its own segment. All the narrowing of the pleuræ is thus effected from the anterior side. The pleural segments are prolonged into flat, acute, recurved spines, with broad contiguous bases; their length is about two-thirds that of the main segments; their inner, concave edges appear to be continuations of the posterior pleural ridges.

Pygidium of moderate size, triangular; axis strong elevated, obconical; with at least two well-impressed transverse furrows near the anterior end, forming there two conspicuous annular lobes, and apparently in some specimens, another faint furrow still farther to the rear. No tubercles detected. The lateral lobes consist of an inner depressed-convex portion, much lower than the axis, traversed by two or three oblique furrows corresponding with the spines, the posterior one, however, quite faint, and a perfectly flat and moderately broad margin from which three flat and acute spines extend backward. These much resemble the pleural spines, but have a less graceful appearance from the tendency of their edges to run into straight lines. The two posterior spines, one on each side, are about as far apart as the width of the axis of the pygidium at its anterior end; the border of the posterior margin which unites them, is nearly or quite a straight line.

Quite a number of specimens have been collected of the glabella and pygidium of this trilobite, in which the features as here described are quite constant. Only one has been found (fig. 5) which exhibits the contour of the complete cephalic shield, and two which show the thoracic segments.

On account of the imperfection of the head and pygidium of the more complete specimen, No. 180 (which I will consider, in any event, the type of the species "*Stissingensis*"), there might be doubt concerning its specific identity with the others. Specimen No. 182 is a link, however, which seems to remove all question from the evidence. The name assigned to the species is that of Mount Stissing, near whose base it occurs.

The close affinity of this trilobite to the type *Olenoides Nevadensis*,* Meek, is very evident and interesting. The main points of difference are: (1) The more slender and tapering thoracic axis. (2) The shape of the axial thoracic segments, and the arrangement of the furrow in these segments. (3) The broad, flat pleural thoracic spinous processes. (4) The different structure of the pygidium.

The glabella and fixed cheeks are also considerably unlike those of "*Ogygia serrula*" Rominger, which Mr. C. D. Walcott, after careful comparison of specimens, considers to be identical with *Olenoides Nevadensis*.† From the calcareous shale, and rarely in the compact limestone.

8. *Discovery of Calciferous Fossils in the Millerton-Fishkill limestone belt; also in a belt near Rhinebeck.*

The Hillsdale-Copake belt of the original Taconic limestone, dividing just south of Copake, enters the northeast corner of

---

* See Bulletin No. 30, U. S. Geological Survey, Plate xxv, fig. 7.
† This Journal, III, vol. xxxvi, 1888, p. 165.

Dutchess Co., in two main belts, the western or Pine Plains—New Hamburg belt, and the eastern, or Millerton-Fishkill belt. Associated with these are a few shorter parallel belts of limestone. The western one has been considerably altered by metamorphic action, but the metamorphic alteration has been much greater in the eastern belt where the limestones are frequently found coarsely crystallized and marble-like, while the associated shales often merge into micaceous or hydro-micaceous schists, or even become gneissoid. These facts were clearly set forth by Professor J. D. Dana, in 1879,* as also the fact that Lower Silurian fossils had been discovered in the western belt, while no definite species of fossils had been made out among the signs of organisms found in the eastern one.

Recently the writer visited the northern end of the Millerton-Fishkill belt, for the first time, in the work of exploration, entering it from the central part of the Shekomeko Valley. The limestone was reached at the eastern base of the high ridge of argillite and micaceous schist which is the southern extension of Winchell Mountains. At once the presence of fossils was discovered in a limestone ledge on the farm of Mr. Edward Clark. The locality is a little less than a quarter of a mile from the village of North East Center, on the Shekomeko road, and scarcely more than one and a half miles, in a straight line, from Millerton railway station. It is about five hundred feet northerly from the road, and but slightly elevated above the surface; the portion exposed is about one hundred and fifty feet long and sixty feet wide, with a strike N. 11° E. (true) and dip 35° westerly.

The rock is a fair sample of the much altered limestone of this eastern belt; its color varies from gray to white, and in many spots it is rather brittle, or inclined to crumble under blows of the hammer. In some cases, where the mass of the rock is grayish, the fossils in it are quite white, making a fine contrast. This fossiliferous limestone is frequently filled with films which very strongly resemble micaceous or hydro-micaceous films; but as I have not had time to examine them carefully I do not venture to assert that they are any other than films of gypsum.

The limestone in this ledge is filled with organic remains, some of which are fairly well defined, appearing in relief on the weathered surfaces;—many of them are distorted by pressure. The so-called Calciferous fucoids are abundant and of the same peculiar forms elsewhere observed in this formation. *Ophileta complanata* (which according to Prof. R. P. Whitfield is identical with *O. compacta*), is present in numerous

---

* This Journal, vol. xvii, May, 1879.

specimens, though not generally well preserved. I obtained four or five good specimens of it about 2¾ centimeters in diameter. Specimens resembling *O. sordida* were observed, but I suspect that they are simply distorted forms of *O. complanata*, as the gain in the size of the whorls is moderate.

An Orthoceras was found, conspicuous in its relief upon the weathered surface. It is about five centimeters long, and one and a third wide; the rate of taper is moderate; the septa number about seven to a centimeter : they are quite oblique, but this may be due to distortion. The siphuncle is two millimeters in diameter; the shape of the cross-section, and position of the siphuncle cannot be known because of the distortion, nor can its species be at present determined. Fragments likely to be those of *Cyrtoceras Vassarina* were also noticed.

No other limestone outcrops were seen in the vicinity, as the rock is extensively covered by drift in this part of the State, though a more careful search would doubtless reveal other localities. Similar fossils were found in adjoining walls indicating a considerable area of the fossiliferous strata. The limestone belt here has a width of about two miles, its eastern edge skirting the base of Indian Mountain in the Connecticut border. Throughout this width there appears to be a general similarity in the lithological characters so far as these could be observed in the rather scarce outcrops. The strata from the village of North East Center are continuous northerly to Millerton and to the north county line, becoming a white and crystalline friable marble in the quarry of the A. H. Maltby furnace, north of Millerton. The belt was also cursorily examined south as far as Amenia, and found to be of a similar character.

These facts show that the Calciferous, which is clearly indicated by the fossils, is at least one of the most prominent components of the Millerton-Fishkill limestone belt. Trenton strata are very likely to be present, but were not observed. No indications of Cambrian strata were noticed between Millerton and Amenia but the search has not yet been thorough. The shales and schists associated with these limestones, and passing sometimes from argillite, without interruption, into hydro-micaceous schist, hold evidently the same stratigraphic position as the shales and schists which are associated with the similar western limestone belts of the county. It is therefore not easy to see how they can be referred to any other horizon than that of the Hudson River Group.

It may be well to announce here that the writer has also found, recently, Calciferous fossils in one of the short belts of limestone lying a few miles east of Rhinebeck village. The fossiliferous locality is at Eighmyville three miles northeast of

Rhinebeck. This limestone has been mentioned by Mr. S. W. Ford, as probably Cambrian, and it contains in considerable quantity what certainly appears like the Potsdam conglomerate of Dutchess and Columbia counties. But the presence of the Calciferous there in a very characteristic form is now beyond doubt.

Note.—Since the above paper was written, Mr. C. D. Walcott's article on the "Position of the Olenellus Fauna," in the July number of this Journal, has been published. In this paper he very justly calls attention to the fact that the fauna here described belongs to the type of the Middle Cambrian of the interior (as of the Rocky Mountain region) rather than to that of the typical Paradoxides of the Atlantic coast; and that, from its position, the Hudson Valley fauna serves in a measure to connect the two.

EXPLANATION OF PLATE VI.

Cambrian Fossils from Stissing, N. Y.

Natural size, except where otherwise noted. All are from the Calcareous shales, except those represented by figs. 5, 6, and 15, which are from the limestones.

Fig. 1. *Hyolithes Billingsi* (?) cast of interior, showing three or four slight annulations; the anterior one more prominent than the others.

Fig. 2. *Leperditia ebenina*, n. sp., enlarged to 2 diameters; fragment of (right?) valve, showing the line of the hinge, and a sloping dorsal angle, also the outer belt of minute contiguous pits, and the inner tract of larger separated pits. The ornamentation indicates that the complete carapace must have been at least one-sixth longer than the fragment.

Fig 3. *L. ebenina* enlarged to 2 diameters: lacking the cardinal margin; showing perfectly the peculiar surface-pitting, and the ventral furrow.

Fig. 4. *L. ebenina*, interior view of a central fragment of a valve; showing the separated tubercles, corresponding to the separated pits of the central exterior.

Enlarged to 2 diameters.

Fig. 5. *Kutorgina Stissingensis*, n. sp., enlarged 2 diameters; a natural cast of the dorsal valve.

Fig. 6. *K. Stissingensis*; enlarged to 2 diameters; ventral valve; with a side view of the elevation.

Fig. 7. Gutta percha cast of a natural impression of the interior of the umbonal region of a ventral valve, referred to *K. Stissingensis*; showing a medial septum from which fine striæ diverge, and muscular impressions, enlarged to 3 diameters.

Fig. 8. *K. Stissingensis*, cardinal view; showing false area, deltidial opening, and the rounded edge between the false area and the main surface of the valve; enlarged to 2 diameters.

Figs. 9. and 10. *Olenoides Stissingensis*, n. sp.; the glabella. Fig. 9 from an artificial cast, Fig 10 with a side view of the elevation.

Fig. 11. *O. Stissingensis*, pygidium.
Fig. 12. *O. Stissingensis*, pygidium, with four attached thoracic segments.
Fig. 13. A free cheek, associated with *O. Stissingensis*.
Fig. 14. Hypostoma of *O. Stissingensis*.
Fig. 15. *O. Stissingensis*, full length, showing eight thoracic segments; details of the glabella obliterated or distorted by compression.

Am. Jour. Sci., Vol. XXXVIII, 1889. Plate VI.

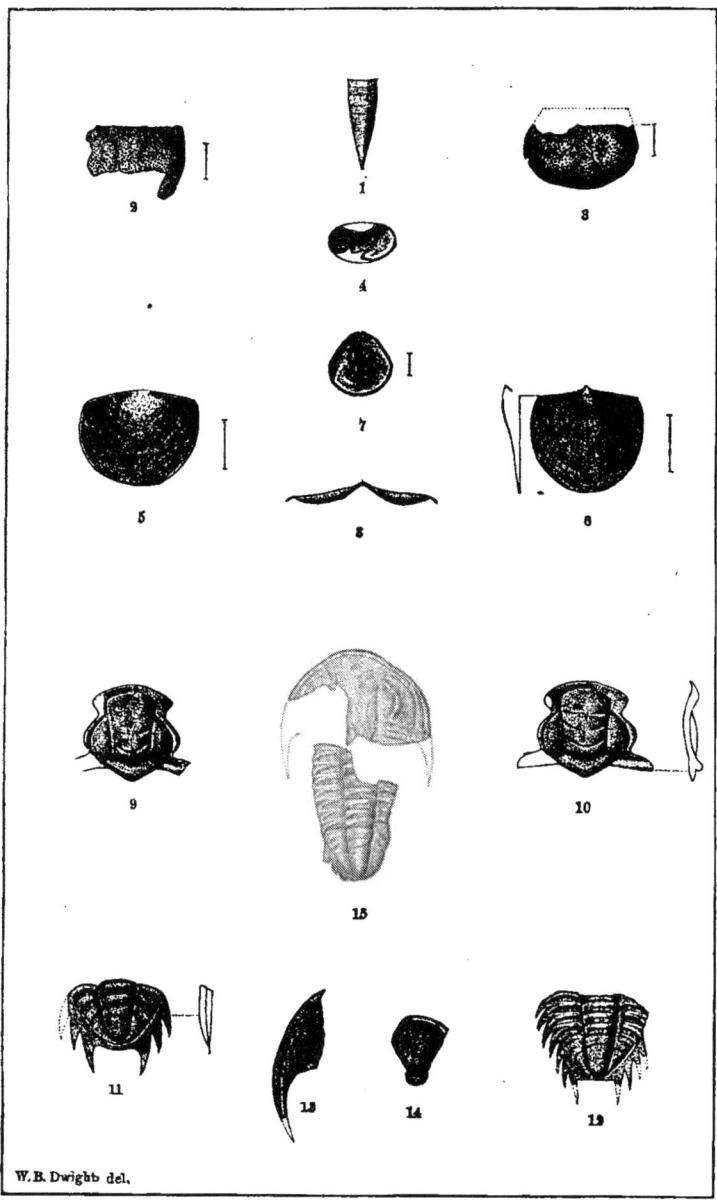

W. B. Dwight del.

Printed by Libri Plureos GmbH in Hamburg, Germany